IT IS WRITTEN
THE SHOCKING DOWNFALL OF THE USA

IT IS WRITTEN
THE SHOCKING DOWNFALL OF THE USA

ROGER H. EWING

authorHOUSE®

AuthorHouse™
1663 Liberty Drive
Bloomington, IN 47403
www.authorhouse.com
Phone: 1-800-839-8640

First published by AuthorHouse   11/24/2009

ISBN: 978-1-4490-5429-8 (e)
ISBN: 978-1-4490-5173-0 (sc)
ISBN: 978-1-4490-5174-7 (hc)

Library of Congress Control Number: 2009912731

Printed in the United States of America
Bloomington, Indiana

This book is printed on acid-free paper.

Dedicated to the American people.

This book is a wake up call to alert Americans that if the United States Congress does not begin to face reality the events of this book may come to pass.

ACKNOWLEDGEMENTS

The author acknowledges utilizing some facts on China from the book, "The Coming Conflict With China" written by Richard Bernstein and Ross H. Munro.

The author acknowledges utilizing facts and quotations from the book, "Why I Left Jihad" written by Walid Shoebat.

The author acknowledges utilizing facts and direct quotes from the Wikipedia, the free encyclopedia.

This book will shock you! If you have a third grade education and you have the ability to think you need to read this book from start to finish. There are ideas in this book you will not agree with based on your knowledge, experiences, and attitude but with the new knowledge in this book if you REALLY THINK about them you will more than likely agree with this author.

This author was one of America's first international inspectors of weapons of mass destruction, WMDs. This author learned about a country's capability to wage war as he participated in the FIRST INTERNATIONAL DISARMAMENT EXERCISE IN 1968. We determined what weapons systems a country had, how many, their capabilities, their manpower, on a daily basis. Every night the host country would move their weapons systems and military personnel anywhere over a 2000 mile area and we had to locate and identify them on a daily basis. My group (group consisted of myself, another officer, and 2 drivers) ended up with the highest efficiency rating of the many groups doing the inspecting and analysis. The results of this study led to the disarmament treaties between the USA and the Soviet Union in the 1970s.

In 1973 this author also successfully predicted the downfall of the Soviet Union to fall from within as it did in 1989. This author predicted the fall from within would happen in 1990.

THIS BOOK, "IT IS WRITTEN THE SHOCKING DOWNFALL OF THE USA", IS A WAKE UP CALL TO ALL AMERICANS. IT IS A CALL TO ACTION.

FIRST, THE UNITED STATES OF AMERICA IS AT WAR WITH ITSELF!

SECOND, THE UNITED STATES OF AMERICA IS AT WAR WITH THE JIHAD!

THIRD, IN A HIGH LEVEL MEETING IN 1994 COMMUNIST CHINA DECLARED THE USA AS THEIR ENEMY NUMBER ONE!

FOURTH, MR. PUTIN IS REBUILDING RUSSIA INTO A DANGEROUS SUPER POWER!

September 11, 2001 seems so long ago to too many Americans. They know a war is going on in the Middle East but for the most part they are not affected and don't feel threatened by it. But, Americans are starting to feel concerned or even threatened by China for several reasons. First, China is a Communist country. Second, Communist China is dramatically increasing its military power and technology. Third, Communist China has become an economic giant.

IT IS WRITTEN that any country that does not prepare to defend itself will be defeated.

Where is the VOICE OF REASON in the USA!

The Korean War (our Congress called it a conflict) was the first test for the USA fighting against the Communist Chinese. The war ended in a draw.

Vietnam gave us the second war involving the Communist Chinese. It officially ended in a draw. Over 50,000 Americans were killed in that war.

The point here that is missed by our politicians the Korean War ended in 1953 and the Communist Chinese had limited technology, and the Vietnam War ended in 1974 and the

Communist Chinese had limited technology yet we could not defeat them. They had mass numbers of military personnel.

In 1994 a large number of Chinese Communist Party officials from all of China's twenty-nine provinces were summoned to a meeting in Beijing. The main address of the meeting was given by Chief of the General Staff Zhang Wannian. General Zhang's central message was " reinforcing the army and accelerating the modernization of the army ". The determination that came out of the meeting was the USA was China's main enemy in the world. The meeting was anti-American.

The collapse of the Soviet Union had enormous implications for Communist China. First it freed Communist China from worrying about the Soviet Union as the Soviet Union had been their number one enemy. Russia by itself did not pose as big a threat. Second, Communist China learned the lesson that political reforms, especially the tolerance of free debate allowed by Mikhail Gorbachev and his willingness to dilute the Russian Communist Party's monopoly on power led to the ousting of the Soviet party altogether.

Also, Communist China learned from the Gulf War. The USA had shown awesome technical power in the Gulf War. The Chinese Communists knew how far behind they were and had to catch up. They vowed to dramatically catch up technically within fifteen years.

Communist China has steadily moved in the direction of being an ally of Russia. In April 1996, Boris Yeltsin and Jiang Zemin signed a declaration of a long term strategic partnership aimed at counterbalancing the USA. Russia has become the chief supplier to China of advanced military equipment and technology, including intercontinental ballistic missiles, advanced SU-27 fighter planes, and kilo-class submarines. In addition, thousands of Russian scientists and technicians are now working directly or indirectly for China's military industries.

China is the world's third largest nuclear power in the number of delivery vehicles in service having surpassed Great Britain and France. Russia is the second largest.

China's nuclear program has included developing and testing missiles with ranges up to eight thousand miles. China's REPORTED GOAL for the year 2000 was to have thirty missiles ready for launch. It is estimated that one hundred plus warheads are targeted on the United States. Eight thousand miles from China reaches the USA. It makes us vulnerable, to say the least.

To say the least the Chinese Communist are building up their military. Their weapons systems are state of the art having recently tested their missile systems by shooting down one of their own satellites. Folks, you need to understand this, the Chinese Communists have dramatically increased their military and have become more aggressive toward the USA and the western world.

Communist China is waiting while the USA is bogged down fighting the terrorists in the Middle East.

No one can change the past. The past is past. It is now time to face the reality. There is plenty of blame to go around and there are no more excuses it is time for action.

This is the moment of truth for Barack Obama. This will finally determine whether Barack Obama's heart is more American than it is Muslim. Remember Barack was born to a Muslim father and lived the first ten years of his life in Muslim countries including going to Muslim schools. So whatever President Obama does or does not do to prepare to defend the USA from imminent destruction which likely will happen during his four years as President. Immediate action is required. The clock is ticking and we are losing ground every day. The stupidity of many has gotten us to this time in history and only he must recognize the blunders and step up to prevent the catastrophic events which are about to strike the USA. This book explains the urgency for immediate action. The year 2010 is the last year to act before the greatest war in history may begin which will culminate in 2012 with over half the world destroyed.

The USA is less prepared for this war than any war we have had to fight. Our American military has been stretched so thin that defeat could come quickly against a formidable foe like Communist China or Russia. They are the big boys we have been fighting against the little countries that didn't have huge armies or military. Look how bogged down we have been. The big boys will wipe us off the face of the map unless we wake up and take immediate action. This is not a game! The only resemblance to a basketball game is that there is a clock and it is ticking and the game ends with a loser.

In this game, Mr. President, you are taking the final shot against Bill Russell in his prime and you need to score to protect the USA nation survival.

Mr. President, why are you and the Congress talking about petty things like getting a government run health care system when our military needs to be increased to five million active duty manpower. You are taking the American people down a path of destruction. If we get defeated by Communist China or Russia, or Muslims no one will have health insurance. You are consumed with changing the USA into a third rate country. You keep talking about that you won the election, well the election is over, its time you became the President of all the people not just President of the unions and the far left. Stand up and do what is right. The game is in the last quarter and we are far behind.

You are not the only one to blame for our being far behind in our defense. Several people have sat in your seat the last 40 years and many have sat in the seats of the Congress and they all share the blame. The American system of re-electing the same rich people to the halls of Washington and their priorities have been for power and re-elections and not doing the work of the American people. You can continue down the same path which leads to destruction or you can lead us in the right direction where the USA can defend itself against the big boys. It takes a man about the size of Bill Russell to stand up to the forces of apathy in Washington.

Where is your heart, Mr. President?

A third grade class was asked to complete the following question, When the population of the USA was 150 million people the active military was at 2 million so now the population is 300 million people how many people should be in the active military? They answered 4 million. Third grade students are 9 years old.

Bill Clinton answered the question by reducing the active military by 25% to one and a half million.

Our Congress obviously does not believe a change is necessary from the one and a half million.

Are the 9 year old kids smarter than our Congress and Bill Clinton? The problem is if they are the American people will find out the hard way when we are attacked.

Our national defense has been like a ping pong ball up and down. Jimmy Carter almost decimated our military. Ronald Reagan built it back up. Then Bill Clinton reduced the active duty personnel by 25%. If there is a problem with a democracy it could be that yo-yo effect with the military. There needs to be long range planning for national defense away from the politics of the moment. The pentagon we may assume does long range planning but it is at the mercy of the Commander-in-Chief. Our national defense needs to be stable. From the actions of the recent Democratic Party Presidents it appears they didn't want a strong military. Hello! How are we going to protect ourselves with a weak military?

The last two people to be in the position of Secretary of Defense were and are "old school". Donald Rumsfeld and Robert Gates both believe that our active duty military is sufficient otherwise they should have spoken up. We needed more manpower from the beginning in Iraq and need more now in several other parts of the Middle East. Politics may become the major cause of our downfall.

The United States of America is considered the richest country in the world. Our population is over 300 million people yet we can afford to keep only one and a half million people on active military duty. When we had 150 million people in the USA we had two million active military. Is there any politician in Washington that sees how illogical this is? We can spend millions and millions and millions of dollars for the Congress representatives for their "pork barrel projects" to get re-elected but they will not spend the money to have the strong military defense that is needed in today's chaotic dangerous world.

The world of 2009 to 2012 is more vulnerable for an all out war then anytime in the history of our planet. World War II in comparison to this next war will seem like it was in the Stone Age.

First, military weapons systems are far more advanced than anything in World War II.

Second, these advanced military weapons systems are in the hands of too many countries including the terrorists groups.

Third, we won't know who is going to be on our side.

Fourth, ever since we were attacked by the Islamic JIHAD Muslim terrorists on September 11, 2001 we have been at war with them. Communist China has declared the USA as their number one enemy. Putin's Russia is waiting.

Fifth, more countries today have nuclear weapons, nuclear bombs, and missiles with nuclear capability than ever before. Just one nuclear weapon going off could ignite World War III.

Sixth, the European countries are relatively weak militarily and many of them don't want to get involved with any war.

READER do you feel safe that we have ONLY one and a half million people in our active military and our potential enemies have probably 10 to 20 million in theirs? The fact that our military has been in Iraq and Afghanistan and we have had to call up our military reserves and national guard just to be where we are today in the war is the problem of having a small military. Many of our military personnel are already on their second and third tours of duty in the war zones.

After Pearl Harbor, in December 1941, we had time to ADD new people into our military. We quickly trained them and several months later they were sent to fight in the war. In the 21st century we would need a year to train the majority of recruits. The technology has become so sophisticated. It would require 6-9 months teaching military computer systems. Another factor everyone would need immediate security clearances to enter the military computer systems. Another question would our young people today line up to join the military like they did in 1941? Or would we need to take the time to institute a draft system?

IF WE WAIT TO BE ATTACKED AGAIN THERE WILL NOT BE ANY TIME TO INSTITUTE A DRAFT SYSTEM. THERE WILL NOT BE THE TIME TO TRAIN ANYONE.

Solution

MY SUGGESTION IS THAT THE CONGRESS OF THE UNITED STATES OF AMERICA IMMEDIATELY INCREASE OUR ACTIVE MILITARY PERSONNEL TO FIVE MILLION.

Our military reserves and national guard should stay within the USA to protect the homeland. That should be their main mission.

THAT THE CONGRESS OF THE UNITED STATES OF AMERICA IMMEDIATELY INSTITUTE A MILITARY DRAFT SYSTEM.

That we do it NOW, and not take a year to set it up.

This is how the draft would work. The Secretary of State of each state obtains a list of all US citizens in their state between the ages of 18 to 35 from the car registrations. A simple computer program puts in the names in alpha order. Then the list is secured. Then five lottery balls are used. The balls are numbered 7 thru 12. A drawing will be on TV where one ball is selected. For example, the ball number 8 is selected. Then every eighth person on the list is selected for the draft and receives a reporting date. The military determines the quota for how many personnel are needed, so many men and so many women. It's SIMPLE AND FAIR! Plus the system can be established in a short period of time. Remember time is of the essence. It takes almost a year to get these recruits ready. Because it takes approximately a year for training the draft is for a period of three years. The draft can be for all the military services – Army, Air Force, Navy, Marines, and Coast Guard.

Now comes the hard part. How do you get the present people in both houses of Congress to pass two bills that is vital to the survival of the United States of America? First, they need to authorize the military to have five million active duty personnel, and second to authorize the draft.

Remember READER our country is divided. Even a subject like survival of our country is party politics. Folks it's ridiculous! The people that are elected to Congress take an oath to defend the USA and in order to defend the USA we must have the proper manpower to do so.

This may not be the "greatest generation" where everyone stood up and contributed like World War II but I have great faith in the American people to stand up and be counted. The division in the USA is caused in large part to the division among the people in both houses of Congress. The national polls of how Congress is doing are below a 20% acceptance level. I think the American people want to survive and will not tolerate their congressman or woman playing games with this most important issue. Survival of our country should be the only issue.

Americans DEMAND A REGISTERED VOTE, for or against, these two bills. Those who oppose these two bills do not have the best interest of the USA and the survival of the

USA. Those who oppose these two bills should be impeached immediately.

The threat of an all out war is more real today than at anytime since World War II.

TERRORISTS ARE EVERYWHERE! WE DON'T KNOW WHERE OR WHEN THEY WILL STRIKE AGAIN. WE NEED TO BE RIGHT 100% OF THE TIME DAY IN AND DAY OUT, YEAR AFTER YEAR. IT'S GOING TO HAPPEN AGAIN.

Not only are the Chinese Communists a military threat but it appears that almost everything you buy in the USA is made in China. It used to be everything was made in Japan. Then everything was made in Taiwan. Amazingly the USA has given Communist China the money to upgrade their technology. How? The USA established Communist China as the manufacturing capital of the world. Today almost every product in a store has a "Made in China" label. The cheap labor force in China and the abundance of it makes for an ideal arrangement for American companies and more importantly their CEOs, Chief Executive Officers, for a quick and short term profit and great balance sheet resulting in a big bonus for them. Many of these American companies reaped huge profits but at the expense of thousands of Americans being laid off. This exporting of work to China and other countries has come at a high price for Americans. Once known as a manufacturer of goods America is now known as a "service economy". There was a report in 1960 that of every 10 jobs in the USA 7 were in manufacturing today that number is one manufacturing job in 10 jobs. There are serious implications associated with this dramatic switch and in the long run it will have a dramatic negative effect on the USA. The effect of American companies building manufacturing plants throughout China to gain cheap labor the past 20 years has backfired. China has become modern. Their people have learned modern day manufacturing methods, systems, and technology.

THE BOTTOM LINE IS THAT COMMUNIST CHINA HAS BECOME A SUPER POWER AT THE EXPENSE OF AMERICA AND AMERICA HAS GOTTEN WEAKER. AMERICA HAS HAD TO BORROW ONE TRILLION DOLLARS FROM CHINA TO KEEP OUR ECONOMY FROM COLLAPSING.

In 1970 President Richard Nixon had his historic meeting with China which opened the door to trade. It is doubtful that anyone knew the explosive results that would follow. At first the Communist Chinese were skeptical of foreigners in their country but as the dollars started adding up they saw the opportunity to come out of the dark ages and become an industrial giant.

In the 1990s American companies using China as their manufacturing part of their business mushroomed. Obviously manufacturing jobs in the USA disappeared proportionally. What did our United States Congress do to prevent this? Nothing! American companies going overseas have helped create a world economy and no one wants to protect American manufacturing jobs to keep them in the USA.

Many Americans are not happy with buying so many of their purchases from China. There have been many recalls of products made in China that do not meet the standards that Americans have become used to. There have been a number of food recalls where the product originated in China. This author was shocked to hear on a major news network broadcast that China supplies over half the wheat in the world. Remember the pet scare. Dog and cat owners all across America were shocked to hear that 90% of the pet food that pet manufactures sold in the USA had wheat gluten that came from China as part of the ingredients. Furthermore, it has been revealed that some of the food in the human food chain also comes from China. It took several months for the food experts in this country to figure out that there was a problem which leads one to question how safe our food really is and how vulnerable our food chain is. What is to prevent poison from entering our human food chain? How long would it take our food experts to act?

Japan inspects 10% of all food imports that they receive from China. Recently they found an appreciable amount of poison in the food imported from China and have questioned the Chinese government. The USA inspects ONLY 1% of the food that is imported from China. That's not much chance to find any poison, is there? Furthermore the USA used to feed the world with our food what happened? Why are we importing so much food from China?

THIS BOOK IS A WAKE UP CALL TO ALL AMERICANS. IT IS A CALL TO ACTION!

THE WAR WITH JIHAD

Notice it's the war with JIHAD not it's the war in Iraq. That applies to Afghanistan and it applies to Pakistan. It applies to any area of the world where the Islamic JIHAD Muslims are attacking the USA and our Allies. This is a CRITICAL POINT. And you need to comprehend this. To do this we need to understand what JIHAD is.

"What JIHAD is: The definition of JIHAD is to fight and kill non-Muslims. It's to call the unbelievers towards the true religion of Islam and to fight against them, if they are unwilling to accept this true religion."

"The Quran orders that non-Muslims must be fought until they believe in Islam."

"Muhammad ordered: Allah's Apostle said, "I have been ordered to fight with the people till they say, none has the right to be worshiped but Allah." Muhammad said, "the earth belongs to Allah and his Apostle."

"Muhammad said," Whoever changes his Islamic religion, kill him."

Folks, the above information in quotation marks is from a former terrorist in the JIHAD movement, Walid Shoebat. Walid Shoebat is in hiding from the JIHAD as they would kill him if they ever found him. Shoebat after studying the Bible in depth had a remarkable transformation to Christianity and he now wants to warn the world about the JIHAD.

Walid Shoebat wrote a book, "Why I Left JIHAD" which details and explains the JIHAD movement which everyone should read.

A little known fact is that Muslims have been killing Jews and Christians for 2000 years. Walid Shoebat in his book, "Why I Left JIHAD" mentions many of the atrocities over the last 2000 years.

Folks, the Muslims who are a part of the JIHAD movement which is estimated to be well over 50% of all Muslims in the world are now more organized and stronger than ever before and their goal is to destroy the USA, Israel, and the Western world. Once the GREAT WAR starts most Muslims of the world will unite. This is a fanatical idea that has been drummed into each Muslim from early childhood and consumes them. Only a very few can escape from this mission.

Islam means "submission" not "peace". Submission to the complete will of Allah (Islamic god) and the duties laid out in the Quran for his followers, and this includes JIHAD.

Shoebat says that the study of the JIHAD is part of all the curriculum of all the Islamic institutes. This study starts in early childhood and ends in the universities.

The prophecy of the Bible states that Jerusalem will be attacked by many nations. The Bible is clear and specific that Muslim nations will attack Jerusalem in the End-time, meaning the end of the world as we know it. Also, any nation that helps divide Jerusalem will be destroyed. That's from the Bible. In 2007 and in 2009 there were and are talks about dividing Jerusalem and the USA is among those nations in talks about doing just that.

(Close to the end of this book the author will explain what happens to Jerusalem and about the NUCLEAR BOMB that may be dropped.)

THE PREDICTIONS FOR 2012

Never have so many different groups predicted the same cata-strophic events for any year in the history of the world as for the year 2012. Folks, search your computer for "predictions for 2012" and you will be in shock of the results. Don't start jumping out of windows or do anything drastic because that prediction MAY be able to be altered. It is noteworthy that these predictions were at different times in history and by different groups independently of each other and in fact did not know of the others predictions.

The Aztecs who predicted many things that came true predicted the world would end in 2012. The Mayans predicted 2012 is the end of time as we know it. IT is written that the next POPE will be the 112th POPE in history and the naming of the 112th POPE will mark the beginning of the end. Also, over 50 years ago this author learned about 2012 when he purchased a book on the GREAT PYRAMID in Egypt. It is well known by many scholars that the GREAT PYRAMID was inspired by GOD as to the layout and construction. It is a stone calendar which has predicted every major event in the world and it ends in 2012! Folks, there are a half dozen other predictions that reveal that 2012 is the critical year. The greatest possibility of that happening is through a nuclear war and we are closer to having a nuclear war than any time in history.

Also, there is the prediction from the BIBLE which was made several thousands of years ago that predicts exactly what will happen when Jerusalem is destroyed. The destruction of Jerusalem may hinge on whether the USA stays in Iraq. (more on this later) We need to change our course right now.

WAKE UP AMERICA !
WE NEED TO TAKE ACTION NOW!

GOD has given mankind the ability to THINK and therefore he has the ability to do RIGHT and that COULD alter the predictions. This book is about changing the course so mankind will do right.

The BIBLE talks about an ALPHA and OMEGA. That means there is a BEGINNING and an END. Folks, the beginning happened thousands of years ago and the end MAY happen soon. The world will not go on forever. The BIBLE is the AUTHORITY on all things. The BIBLE is the WORD of GOD.

UNBELIEVABLE EVENT

Folks, an unbelievable event happened in the world in 1776 as GOD had HIS hand on a remarkable group of men who were willing to sacrifice everything including their lives to form a country, a REPUBLIC, and create "something" called DEMOCRACY. As we all know today these remarkable men succeeded and the UNITED STATES OF AMERICA was born. The odds of that happening were astronomical and it happened only because GOD had HIS hand on the events that made that possible. And GOD has blessed the USA ever since. Religion played a major part in GOD establishing the USA as the people of that time wanted to serve GOD. GOD must have made a covenant with the USA that as long as the American people served HIM and became the protector of the world HE would bless her. But Americans increasingly are going away from GOD and from wanting to meet their global responsibilities. There has been and will continue to be a price to pay for this. Americans must wake up to reality that we can not hide from the world as we did during the Clinton years in the White House because that led to several hundred Americans being killed by Muslims and to the 9/11 attacks. We can not retreat and surrender our role in the world and expect to win or be left alone as the enemy will attack again and again as we found out under Clinton. Folks, the predictions for 2012 are real and we need to alter the course of self indulgence and become responsible again as individuals and as a nation and stop the insanity of wanting to withdraw from our GOD given duty in Iraq and the Middle East. If Americans do not honor GOD the USA will fall from within.

It's a WAR between the USA and its ALLIES against the Islamic JIHAD terrorists. Some of these JIHAD terrorists have called this WORLD WAR III. The Islamic JIHAD terrorists have repeatedly stated their goal to DESTROY THE USA.

Why aren't we Americans listening? Why aren't we concerned? One explanation is that this war has ONLY affected our active military, our military reserves, and National Guard units and their respective families. There are one and a half million in our active military. The reserves and the National Guard units approximate another two million plus their families. So approximately five million people are directly affected out of over 305 million. The rest of the country about 300 million people go about their daily lives without any sacrifice. Of the 300 million most know there is a war going on from watching television, the internet, or occasionally reading a newspaper.

A small group of people that we call the US Congress knows there is a war on as many of them love to be seen on television.

President George W. Bush, while still in office, had finally said that this war may be for the survival of the USA. But it is the POLITICS of the current US Congress that has divided the American people and has prevented an overwhelming high percentage of Americans from realizing and accepting the fact that this war is for survival and the survival of the USA. With half the US Congress saying this is NOT a war against terrorists it is confusing to all who will listen to them.

After all, why should the 300 million Americans worry as they have the 5 million Americans worrying for them and doing their work. And the United States of America is the greatest military power in the history of the world.

If history has proven anything over the last 5000 years, it is the fact that history repeats itself. History reveals that ALL of the greatest military powers of the last 5000 years were defeated. The great Chinese empire, the great Greek empire, the great Roman empire, Cyrus and the great Persian empire, and possibly the greatest of them all Alexander the Great and the Macedonians, each was the greatest military power up to their time in history. Each was confident that their dominance would last forever. The Greek "Congress" and the Roman "Congress" have been characterized just like our current US Congress. The selfishness of many of the members and the continuous infighting divided the empire and as we all know Greece and Rome fell from within. When the enemy came they were undecided and weren't ready and they were defeated and destroyed.

The author assumes the reader is knowledgeable about the past great empires of the world and the history of the world and does not need to elaborate.

THE US CONGRESS OF 1941 – 1945 STOOD UP TO THEIR RESPONSIBILITY. THEY SOMEHOW KNEW THEY HAD TO DEFEND THE WORLD FROM GERMANY AND JAPAN. ALSO, ALMOST EVERY AMERICAN RESPONDED IN SOME WAY TO CONTRIBUTE TO THE DEFENSE OF OUR COUNTRY AND TO THE EVENTUAL VICTORY. (The author assumes the reader is knowledgeable about the contributions of so many Americans.)

THIS IS CALLED THE GREATEST GENERATION!

Today in 2010 Nancy Pelosi, Harry Reid, General Murtha, Henry Waxman, Barney Frank, Joe Biden, and President Barrack Obama run the country. They will stick to a timetable and no matter what happens the Americans will come home. Then another phase of this war will begin.

WILL THIS BE THE WEAKEST GENERATION? WILL THIS BE THE LAST GENERATION THAT AMERICANS WILL GOVERN THE USA?

AMERICANS AND ESPECIALLY THE LEADERS OF THE USA NEED TO COME TO GRIPS WITH REALITY BEFORE IT IS TOO LATE.

It is said that the terrorists are invisible but make no mistake they are being sponsored by several countries. Those several countries are WAITING for the Americans to leave Iraq.

Before the war the Republicans and the Democrats received all the intelligence that was available. All of our Allies had the same intelligence. Saddam Hussein worked very hard to fake the strength of his military and whatever weapons he had because he was afraid Iran was going to attack him. After all,

Iraq and Iran recently completed a 10 year war. So Saddam Hussein set up mobile weapon carriers that moved around Iraq and American satellites picked it up and the analysis indicated from way up in the sky that he had weapons of mass destruction. After all Iraq had some previously. The intelligence became overwhelming. Both the Republicans and the Democrats believed that there was no other choice but to go to war. The most honorable man, Secretary of State Colin Powell, even went to the United Nations and convinced them.

It is only because the war has dragged on that we are in a situation that appears hopeless. George Washington was in a similar situation. Remember? Yes, the George Washington, Father of our country. His "army" was a bunch of rag tag men who were poorly trained, unequipped, unfed, inexperienced, and vastly outnumbered. Their chances of success were hopeless, a long shot. But somehow he kept his small group together and enough men stuck with him and John Adams believed in him and Adams kept enough members of the newly formed Congress believing in him. As we all know George Washington and his men finally won a battle. And they won another battle and another battle until they won the war – AGAINST ALL ODDS!

In the meantime, the newly formed Congress was working on writing a constitution. And it was frustrating and confusing as days turned into weeks and weeks into months and months into years. Many times the leaders of the states were ready to give up and go home in defeat. We all know the great contributions of Thomas Jefferson and Benjamin Franklin but perhaps the greatest contribution came from John Adams. It was John Adams that kept these great independent thinking men from the 13 colonies together and HE WOULD NOT let them give up. Also, it was John Adams who encouraged support and drummed up food and supplies for George Washington and his band of followers that was loosely called an army. As we all know these men stuck together and succeeded and wrote a constitution, the Constitution of the United States of America. And what a CONSTITUTION it was and still is. What an achievement against all odds! We had the right men at the right time. The only time in the history of the United States of America that we had four great American leaders at the same time was at the beginning when our history needed all four of them. These four, John Adams, Benjamin Franklin, Thomas Jefferson, and George Washington, built the foundation which was to become the greatest country in the world. Also, credit for many of the principles written in our Constitution should go to a preacher named Roger Williams who landed on Plymouth Rock in 1620 and eventually established his church in Rhode Island.

It's fair to say that when Thomas Jefferson wrote most of the Constitution he took from Roger Williams. Also, must note that Ben Franklin was the source of wisdom and knowledge of his time. I doubt very seriously that today's Congress made up of 50 states and more people in Congress could come up with a Constitution much less a great achievement like our founding fathers.

Another great example of hopelessness and against all odds was our civil war of 1861—1865. The right man was there for the USA, Abraham Lincoln. Against all odds Abe Lincoln kept our country together. Very few people stood with Abe Lincoln but he was so determined. As we all know Lincoln persevered and won.

Another great example of fighting against all odds was President Teddy Roosevelt. Not only was Teddy a war hero but his fight was against the largest corporations in the country that had a monopoly in the major industries. Teddy Roosevelt won that fight.

Other great notable American men were General George Patton, General Charles MacArthur, General Dwight Eisenhower, and Ronald Reagan.

THE UNITED OF AMERICA HAS UP TO NOW BEEN EXTREMELY FORTUNATE THAT

WHEN WE NEEDED A MAN OF CHARACTER AND LEADERSHIP WE HAVE HAD SUCH A MAN OR MEN.

In 2010 who will step up in our time of need? Who has the character and leadership to make a difference for the good of the USA? The following are some candidates:

America's Mayor Rudy Giuliana -- has the honor, character, and leadership but ran a poor campaign for president.

Senator Joe Lieberman – has the honor and character, probably the most respected politician in Washington.

Newt Gingrich – had a great run in leading the Congress to success, has been working on solutions for USA.

Sarah Palin – has the honor, character, and leadership to make a difference, but has had her character FALSELY assassinated.

Hillary Clinton – ONLY if she comes out and says she disagrees with Barrack Obama's policies and resigns her position as Secretary of State in 2010. She must say she is smarter and stronger for the experience. She now has more courage to do what is right for our country. But if Hillary stays the four years under Obama she will be branded as too liberal and perceived as agreeing with his policies.

THE MIDDLE EAST, INDIA, AND ASIA

In order to understand the Middle East we need to understand how the present day countries in that region evolved. The one common thread running through the region was the British Empire which was the largest empire in history and for a time was the foremost global power. It was a product of the European age of discovery, which began with the maritime explorations of the 15th century, that sparked the era of the European colonial empires.

By 1921, the British Empire held sway over a population of about 458 million people, approximately one-quarter of the world's population. It covered about 36.6 million km (14.2 million square miles), about a quarter of Earth's total land area. As a result, its legacy is widespread, in legal and governmental systems, economic practice, militarily, educational systems, sports, and in the global spread of the English language. At the peak of its power it was often said that, "the sun never sets on the British Empire" because its span across the globe ensured that the sun was always shining on at least one of its numerous colonies or subject nations.

The British Empire included parts of the following:

1. Africa
2. North America
3. Central America and the Caribbean
4. South America
5. Antarctic Region
6. Asia
7. Atlantic
8. Europe
9. Indian Ocean
10. Australia and the Pacific

The British Empire ruled and or administered parts of the Middle East and India from 1858 to 1947. This part of the empire was called the British Indian Empire. It included the regions of present day India, Pakistan, and Bangladesh and several others but at different times including Burma, Somaliland, Singapore, and Iraq. Egypt was not a part of the British Indian Empire but was occupied and ruled by the British Empire from 1801 to 1922. Egypt received its independence in 1922. On August 14, 1947 at midnight the British Empire gave India its independence and created the Dominion of Pakistan for the Muslims out of India. The official ceremonies taking place first in Pakistan on the 14th and the next day on the 15th in India. Pakistan was divided into two separate areas, West Pakistan and East Bengal (East Pakistan).

PAKISTAN

West Pakistan, it was widely perceived, dominated politically and exploited the East economically, leading to many grievances. The situation reached a climax when in 1970 the Awami League, the largest East Pakistani political party, led by Sheikh Mujibur Rahman, won a landslide victory in the national elections. The party won 167 of the 169 seats allotted to East Pakistan and thus a majority of the 313 seats in the National Assembly. This gave the Awami league the constitutional right to form a government. However, Zulfikar Ali Bhutto the leader of the Pakistan Peoples Party in West Pakistan, refused to allow Rahman to become the Prime Minister. On March 25, 1971 the West Pakistan military in a violent crackdown on East Pakistan led to Indian support for the insurgency leading to the Indo-Pakistani War of

1971. The Indian military and the East Pakistanis decisively defeated the West Pakistani forces deployed in the East. The war resulted in East Pakistan's independence as the new nation of Bangladesh.

Folks, you may have noticed the name Bhutto. The Bhutto family was a prominent Muslim Family. Sir Shah Nawaz Bhutto in 1947 was a controversial figure in a palace coup in the state of Junagadh (now in Gujarat). He was the cofounder of the Sindh Peoples Party in 1934. He was one of the wealthiest and most influential landowners of Sindh and was a good friend of the Governor General (later president) Iskander Mirza. His son, Zulfikar Ali Bhutto, also became a controversial figure. He talked about democracy but his actions were against it as another political party won the election and he would not allow them to form a government. This action resulted in the minds of many including the former leader of Pakistan, Pervez Musharaf, in the crisis which led to the Bangladesh Liberation War. Zulfikar had gained power and influence by becoming a trusted advisor to President Muhammed Ayub Khan who had seized power and declared marital law. Then after gaining popularity and founding the Pakistan Peoples Party he began opposing Ayub Khan and forced him to resign. He became President of Pakistan. He became criticized for intimidating his political opponents and eventually was executed. After her husband's execution, his wife Nusrat Bhutto became the leader of the Pakistan Peoples Party. But she was soon eclipsed by her daughter, Benazir Bhutto, who became Prime Minister. Benazir had two brothers. A number of the Pakistani people believed she had a hand in killing her brothers as both of them did not approve of her corrupt ways of running Pakistan.

A Pakistani military coup in 1999 resulted with General Pervez Musharraf assuming executive powers. Musharraf became President. Benazir Bhutto was assassinated during the February 2008 election campaign. Yousaf Raza Gillani from the Pakistan Peoples Party became Prime Minister. Musharraf resigned from the presidency when faced with impeachment.

Pakistan is the sixth most populous country in the world with 181 million people and has the second largest Muslim population in the world after Indonesia. The population of Indonesia is 222 million. Pakistan has the second largest Shia Muslim population in the world. Pakistan has had many changes of government in the last thirty years making it one of the most unstable countries in the world. A major problem is that Pakistan has a reported 50 to 100 nuclear weapons and they need to be secured.

AFGHANISTAN

Over the centuries waves of migrating peoples passed through the region which is today called Afghanistan. Vast armies of the world passed through this region of Asia temporarily establishing local control and often dominating ancient Afghanistan. Most of Afghanistan's history was spent as part of the larger events that took place upon the Iranian plateau as a whole. It is not surprising that it is the Iranic past and Islamic invasions of the Arabs that have defined modern Afghanistan. It was not until 1747 when Ahmed Shah Durrani founded the monarchy that ruled the country until 1973. Durrani consolidated chieftains, principalities, and fragmented provinces into one country. All of the rulers during this period were from the Durrani's Pashtun tribal confederation.

After some years of political corruption and poor economic conditions a Soviet backed political party, the PDPA, in a bloody coup overthrew the ruling family and came to power in 1978. The PDPA, People's Democratic Party of Afghanistan, instituted Marxist reforms. The Afghan people led by "holy Muslim warriors", Mujahideen, began uprising against the Soviet Union which led to the Soviet army invasion and continued fighting that lasted until 1989. The USA, Pakistan, and Saudi Arabia assisted in the financing the Afghan mujahideen rebels.

Folks, for the record this war started during President Jimmy Carter's term in office.

After the Soviets pulled out civil war broke out among various factions. A group called the Taliban took control of approximately 95% of the country by the end of 2000. The opposition formed the Afghan Northern Alliance which continued to receive diplomatic recognition in the United Nations as the government of Afghanistan.

Folks, for the record the Taliban took control of Afghanistan in the 1990s during President's Bill Clinton term in office. Why did Bill Clinton allow the Taliban to take control of Afghanistan? Was this the critical moment in history when we could have stopped the Taliban? In fairness to Bill Clinton he was busy with that young intern! That was much more pleasurable than protecting the world from evil.

After several Muslim attacks against the USA during Clinton's term in office without any sign of any American retaliation the Muslim world regarded the USA soft. That led to Al Qaida's attack on the USA on September 11, 2001. After 9/11 the Taliban supported Al Qaida.

Then the USA and its coalition allies launched an invasion of Afghanistan to oust the Taliban.

Sponsored by the UN, Afghan factions chose Hamid Karzai, a Pashtun, to be their leader for two years. In October 2004 Karzai was elected as President of Afghanistan in the country's first ever presidential election.

IRAQ

The Ottoman Empire ruled most of the territory of present day Iraq from 1533 to 1918 except for a period of 90 years when the Mamluk officiers of Georgian origin took control. The Ottoman Empire defeated the Mamluk regime and again controlled Iraq.

The Ottoman Empire sided with Germany and the Central Powers in World War I. British forces were instrumental in defeating them and captured Bagdad in 1917.

Iraq was carved out of the Ottoman Empire by the French and British as agreed in the Sykes-Picot Agreement. In 1920 it became a League of Nations mandate under British control with the name "State of Iraq".

Britain imposed a Sunni Hashimite monarchy on Iraq and defined the territorial limits. Emil Faisal, leader of the Arab revolt against the Ottoman sultan during World War I, and a member of the Sunni Hashimite family with the influence of T. E. Lawrence became the first king of the new state.

In 1958 the Hashimite monarchy was overthrown by the military and the new government became a monarchy. After a period of instability the Ba'ath Party took power in 1968 with Ahmed Hasan al-Bakr becoming President and Chairman of the Revolutionary Command Council (RCC). In 1979 al-Bakr resigned naming Saddam Hussein his successor. Territorial disputes with Iran in 1980 led to the Iran –Iraq War (1980-1988).

Iraq invaded Kuwait in 1990.

In January 1991, with the approval of the United Nations 28 countries led by the USA struck Iraq in a war that lasted six weeks and became known as Desert Storm. Iraq was soundly defeated and agreed to leave Kuwait.

Then after years of not complying with the United Nations Resolutions the USA and the United Kingdom invaded Iraq in March 2003.

SAUDI ARABIA

People of various cultures have lived in what is now Saudi Arabia over 5000 years. The rise of Islam in the 620s AD and the subsequent religious importance of the Arabian cities of Mecca and Medina, two of the holiest places in Islam, have given the rulers of this territory significant influence.

The first Saudi state was established in 1744 and lasted until 1818 as the House of Saud with other allies became the dominant state in Arabia controlling most of Nejd. The Ottoman Empire reconquered it in 1818. But the House of Saud returned to power in 1824 and ruled until 1891. In 1891 they were defeated by the Al Rashid dynasty of Ha'il. In 1902 Abdul Aziz Ibn Saud defeated the Al Rashid family and continued on by defeating several enemies until 1926 when he controlled all of Nejd and Hejaz. In January 1926 he became King Abdul Aziz of the kingdom of Hejaz and Nejd. In 1932 the United Kingdom recognized the independence and these regions became unified as the Kingdom of Saudi Arabia.

The House of Saud still rules Saudi Arabia.

THE OTTOMAN EMPIRE

The Ottoman Empire was a multi-ethnic and multi-religious Turkish state. At the height of its power in the 16th and 17th centuries it spanned three continents. It controlled much of Southeastern Europe, the Middle East, and North Africa. It controlled 29 provinces. The empire was at the center of interactions between the eastern and western worlds for six centuries. The Ottoman Empire was an Islamic successor to the earlier Mediterranean empires, namely the Roman and Byzantine empires.

The Ottoman Empire began in 1299 and ended in 1922.

ISRAEL AND PALESTINE

Going back 3500 years the land that is now Israel was called Palestine but was occupied primarily by Jews. This land was in the center of continuous invasions by many different groups. The amazing fact that the Jews survived as a people can only be attributed to God as they were massacred numerous times. The Jews are HIS chosen people and the USA and all countries of the world need to recognize this. Jerusalem and Israel needs to be protected according to the WORD of GOD. Not if, but when the Muslims/JIHAD attack that may signal the beginning of the End-Time.

TO CONTINUE TO GIVE AWAY MORE LAND TO THE TERRORISTS/MUSLIMS/JIHAD IS TO QUICK-EN THE BEGINNING OF THE END.

BRIEF SYNOPIS OF THIS SECTION

The brief histories of the countries mentioned is to show how these countries evolved and what influences they had along the way to them becoming who and what they are today.

One thing that stood out in studying these countries which is not mentioned in their brief histories was the fact that a number of times when a ruler attempted to establish democratic reforms he was overthrown or assassinated. Many of these countries are the cradle of civilization, the beginning of time, and to change their form of government is a mammoth undertaking quite possible requiring generations to accomplish.

For example, former President George W. Bush was committed to turning modern day Iraq into a democracy. The

2007/2008 US Congress controlled by the Democrats expected instant political results in Iraq. Only after the USA and its Allies have gained military superiority and control can the Iraqi politicians feel somewhat secure in doing the work they need to do. The Democrats kept saying they need a political solution in Iraq now. But these Democrats who want instant gratification in Iraq cannot solve their problems in the USA. Immigration has been a problem in the USA for twenty years and nothing has been done. Oil dependency has been a problem in the USA since 1973 and the problem has only gotten worse as today we are more dependent on oil than ever before. Health care has been a problem for many years in the USA and nothing has been done. That's pure nonsense from our career politicians whose only priority is to live the good life and get re-elected. That third grade class could not have done any worse!

So why should we expect a new democracy like Iraq to achieve their goals in such a short period of time especially in a war where the politicians are threatened with their life? A politician in Iraq is not only under heavy political pressure to vote a certain way on an issue but also he or she could be killed for voting. Imagine for a minute if the American politicians were under that pressure that by voting he or she could be killed. Folks that is pressure! The two leading Democratic candidates for the 2008 presidential election, Barrack Obama and Hillary Clinton, have shown poor judgement and a lack of understanding of the grave consequences that can happen to an Iraqi politician in demanding a quick solution to all of Iraq's problems. Wonder how many of our current American politicians would choose to be a politician if they feared for their life just by being an elected politician? For Barrack Obama and Hillary Clinton to have said that no progress has been made in Iraq and that every item in the Iraq Commission report has to be met to have success was absurd. Furthermore, the Iraq Commission report may have included some items that in theory can not be met or should not be met. In addition, the authors of the Iraq Commission report may have had some personal bias.

Playing politics with the security of the USA for the sake of being elected or re-elected should be a crime. Folks, a politician in the USA can not be held accountable for his or her actions/words and has a free will to do as they please. The only accountability is that they can be defeated in the next election, or censored (which happens in rare extremes cases), or assassinated (which has not happened for some time). Folks, this author is in favor of cleaning up politics. For example, if a politician lies to the American people during a campaign or while in office that lie when proven should be at least equal to that politician having lied to a grand jury and should be immediately sentenced to at least five years in prison.

Folks let's restore honesty and integrity in Washington. If athletes are considered role models then members of congress should also be in the same class especially since they are older and supposedly more mature.

Politics Trumps Reality Harmful to our Country?

The author previously mentioned some mistakes Bill Clinton made well George W. Bush made some major mistakes as well.

In his first term in office former President George W. Bush had an advantage in Congress which he floundered away. Remember the Republicans controlled the Congress. The top two priorities should have been the war and securing our borders. It's logical to think that since we were attacked on 9/11 we should do all in our power to keep any more terrorists out of our country and therefore secure our borders. President George W. Bush and the Congress did very little to secure our borders. Yes, finally legislation was passed but not much has been done. The border issue was and still is an immediate issue. President George W. Bush spent his political capital on an issue that is 20/30 years away – social security. Experts reported that the social security system is solvent until 2041! Reasonable Americans will forever question why so little has been done about securing our borders. (President Obama in his first year in office has not begun to secure our borders either) This issue along with the ineffective and insecure Generals have been the large factors why many Americans, Democratic and Republican, have changed their mind about Bush's handling of the war. Americans will support the Commander-in Chief when a war is going badly but when it is conceived that the leadership is flawed then support begins to wane. It wasn't until Senator John McCann kept pestering everybody that more military manpower was needed that the war shifted and a great surge resulted.

Another major mistake right after 9/11 was the Democratic leadership. Senator Daschle who had been a successful majority leader lost his way and he was defeated. Along came Senator Harry Reid of Nevada who at this critical point in American history and who should have learned something from watching Senator Daschle could have become a great statesman. The country finally came together after 9/11 and politics as usual of party bickering should have given way to rallying together. When the Democrats took control of Congress during Bush's second term the power rushed to their heads and the country was further divided. A Senate Majority leader has the distinction of rallying his party and for that matter the country into achieving honorable goals. But Senator Harry Reid chose to play puppet to the new Speaker of the House Nancy Pelosi.

So Pelosi and Reid became the opposition, they calling for the withdrawal of American troops from Iraq. Nancy Pelosi "got the power" and being a woman liked a man in uniform with a "star' on his collar and she completely accepted whatever General John Murtha said. Therefore whatever General Murtha said became the gospel of Nancy Pelosi and the Democratic Party. All three, Murtha, Pelosi, and Reid, showed a lack of support and respect for the American men and women fighting the war. It's a sensitive subject but there are TACTFUL WAYS of opposing a war in progress where 130,000 American lives are at stake and fighting their all every day and all have been TACTLESS at times. Politics aside, that speaks volumes about their character!

The Democratic Party call for the Iraqis to step up and take over the defense of their country in 2005, 2006, 2007, and 2008 was and still is premature. The reality is that the Iraqis are stepping up and the Iraqi military is doing all that they know how to do. How many times have you watched television news and heard that a group of Iraqis standing in line to sign up for the army were killed? If you watch enough news you have heard this many times. The problem isn't that the

Iraqis don't want to defend their country because they do and they are dying every day as proof. The Iraqis need the right leadership to mold all of the politicians from the various factions of a very divided country which has a further complex of independent sheiks who rule their little areas and all is subject to an Al Qaeda attack at any minute to stir up even more problems for those who are trying to govern.

REALITY IS UNDERSTANDING WHAT IS GOING ON. WHAT IS REAL!

What is real in American politics? Anyone who watches an unbiased news report can see the reality. Too many people in Congress are so self serving that that becomes their agenda, their reality. Many of these people have had several terms in Congress. Most didn't have to spend the millions of dollars of their own money it took to get them into Congress and somehow many have found a way to get rich while being there. And they want to continue being there. Wouldn't you? This is the private agenda of many of our self serving Congressional men and women. They don't do the work that the American people elect them to do.

This is a good reason to have TERM LIMITS FOR CONGRESS!

My suggestion is for twelve years total. A Senator may have two terms and a Representative may have six terms. They may have a combination but not to exceed twelve years total.

The public agenda of many of our Congressional men and women is to find a rallying cry that if they bunch together and yell it often enough the American people will start believing what they hear. The rallying cry during the George W. Bush administration in this case was simple, rally against President Bush. What appeared to too many free thinking Americans was it was more important for the leaders of the opposition to defeat President Bush than to do what was right for America. Let us not forget that most of these Congressional men and women voted for the war. President Bush gave the Generals the manpower and the tools they requested to win the war. The Generals plan the strategy and prepare the military to fight to win. Every President is at the mercy of the Generals he inherits. Remember, General Casey was in charge for the first two and a half years and he did not believe in the surge when it finally happened.

An important issue that is rarely mentioned in the media was that the "approval rating" of the Congress was lower than that of President Bush during the mid term election of 2006 that gave the Democrats control of Congress. The people voted against a Congressional man or woman for their stand on issues, including local issues, not necessarily against the war or for bringing the troops home. The Democrats represented the vote and victory for personal issues of bringing the troops home.

Some of these Congressional men and women called for negotiation, a political settlement but they did not know with whom this negotiation or political settlement would be with. What negotiation or political settlement could the USA make with Al Qaeda or JIHAD? Al Qaeda/JIHAD will fight until they win or are destroyed. They will go underground and fight another day. Remember, Harry Reid, the Democratic Senate majority leader said, "the war was lost". Did he want to negotiate a surrender? Folks, the people in the Congress are not the smartest people that we have in the country.

THE JIHAD

Americans must understand that September 11, 2001(now commonly called 9/11) was NOT an isolated event. Islamic JIHAD terrorists have been terrorizing various parts of the world for over 30 years (2000 years but mention 30 here to be more realistic for Americans). When Osama bin Laden emerged as their accepted leader terrorism became more organized and centralized. JIHAD has become a way for millions of followers of the Islamic religion. 98% percent of the Islam religion is made of Muslims. In some Muslim countries children at the age of five years old go to school are taught to hate Americans and the western ideas.

Muslims are all over the world. Muslims are in India which has a population of one BILLION people the second most populated country in the world next to China. China's population is one BILLION three hundred million. The most Muslim populated country in the world is Indonesia.

Muslims are also in Pakistan, Iran, Syria, Iraq, Afghanistan, Lebanon, Saudi Arabia, Palestine, Egypt, Jordan, Kuwait, Morocco, Turkey, and throughout parts of Europe. Great Britain, Germany, France, and Spain each have a Muslim presence. Many other countries have a Muslim presence including the USA with three million people.

Of these predominantly Muslim countries India and Pakistan are considered to have NUCLEAR WEAPONS. India is considered to be on the side of the USA and the WEST. India is surrounded by Muslim countries that are not necessarily friendly to the USA. Pakistan's leadership purports to be on the side of the West but is considered by many to be somewhat unstable.

Since 1948 the Muslim world has had a rallying point as Israel became a country. Israel has been in the middle of the Middle East conflict since its inception. Israel has been supported by the USA and the West, and has NUCLEAR WEAPONS. Up to now Israel has held its own against Muslim attacks and even won a few wars.

But the war of 2006 between Israel and Hezbollah was a preview of things to come. Hezbollah with money, weapons, and even some manpower from Iran put up a stiffer fight than expected by most experts. Hezbollah is controlled by Iran. Iran is Shiite and Hezbollah is Shiite. Iran finances Hezbollah.

The Iranian leaders tested Israel to gain information on the military strength and will of the Jewish leaders and people. They also tested their weapons systems for effect, accuracy, and range. Iran now knows what improvements they need to make. They Iran has bought more weapons systems form Russia, China, and North Korea and upgraded the technology. Therefore, Hezbollah has been rearmed. Hezbollah is now in many countries with terrorists cells throughout the world. Hezbollah is militarily stronger than Al Qaeda.

Israel may be in trouble militarily the next time around and to further weaken Israel there are negotiations underway to return parts of Jerusalem to the Muslims. Even the USA is considering it. Jerusalem is the "SPIRITUAL CAPITAL OF THE WORLD". Remember your BIBLE the WORD OF GOD. THE LORD GOD SAID MANY NATIONS WILL GO AGAINST JERUSALEM AND THOSE THAT PARTICIPATE IN THE DESTRUCTION OF JERUSALEM WILL BE DESTROYED. By being the major influence in the world allowing parts of Jerusalem to be returned to the Muslims the USA is subject to being destroyed. GOD RULES!

Walid Shoebat said it's not about the land! The USA has pressured Israel in giving up some of its land to the Muslims over the years, the land that GOD gave to Israel. But no matter how much land the Muslims receive the JIHAD takes control and their goal remains the same and that is to destroy Israel. President Barrack Obama has put more pressure on Israel than any previous administration. Remember Obama was born to a Muslim father. For the first time since 1948 Israel is concerned that the USA will not support them.

Somewhere between Afghanistan and Pakistan is Osama bin Laden's Al Qaeda headquarters. Al Qaeda's headquarters still has some important terrorists including Al-Zawahiri who is running the operations since Osama bin Laden is dead. Sylvia Brown who can see these things and has an undisputable record of being correct said this on national television. That's right! The recent tapes of Osama are fake. We may never be able to prove it as there are thousands of places where they could have hid his body in those mountains and caves.

Senator Joe Lieberman said on June 10th, 2007 that 90% of Americans killed in Iraq recently were at the hands of Iranian trained Iraqi terrorists with ties to Al Qaeda. Senator Lieberman further said that we should stop Iran from killing Americans by attacking their terrorist camps along the border.

This is a complex world with fragile relationships. On top of the problems with some of the Muslim countries China and Russia have supported and defended Iran in the United Nations. And we can't forget North Korea and Venezuela.

Some people have said that Iraq is another Vietnam. You be the judge. What's the difference between Vietnam and Iraq? Vietnam started in 1959 and ended in 1975. President Eisenhower sent American "advisors" into Vietnam to help the French in 1959. The French had been fighting in Vietnam for years. Eisenhower left office in 1960. President Kennedy in 1961 sent American troops to Vietnam and by the time President Lyndon Johnson left office there were 450,000 Americans fighting in Vietnam. Over 50,000 Americans died in the Vietnam War. By contrast NO TERRORIST GROUP ATTACKED THE USA TO START OR INVOLVE THE USA INTO THE VIETNAM WAR. The Iraqi war started on the intelligence that Saddam had weapons of mass destruction and he was connected to Al Qaeda and we were responding from the attack on 9/11. A story that has recently been made public by an Iraqi who was close to Saddam said that Saddam wanted the world to believe that he had weapons of mass destruction because he wanted to appear strong. Saddam feared that if he appeared weak Iran would attack him and as we all know Iran and Iraq just completed a long war several years earlier and this was a reasonable assumption understanding the history of the two countries. There is some proof that Saddam had some WMDs at least according to a Syrian General who claimed that after Saddam's military was defeated by the USA that prior to the war these WMDs were moved to Syria. Also, to further complicate the evidence of going after Saddam some important leaders of Al Qaeda were spotted in Bagdad prior to the war. Folks, what were reasonable men and women to think?

Did you notice the difference of 450,000 to 130,000 military personnel? The enemy in Iraq is as powerful as the enemy was in Vietnam. The number of enemy in Iraq is also as large as it was in Vietnam. The Iraqi war it appears is more complicated as there are several more factions involved. The factions include the Shiites, Sunni, Kurds, Al Qaeda, Iranians, Hezbollah, Syrians, and the American side. Somehow 130,000 American military personnel are asked to do what 450,000 couldn't do. The author does not see much resemblance, do you?

But what happened when the Americans pulled out of Vietnam and Cambodia? We were also in Cambodia. OVER THREE MILLION PEOPLE MOSTLY VIETNAMESE WERE KILLED, ANNIHILATED! THE SOUTH VIETNAMESE WERE OVERRUN AND SURRENDERED. WHY DID WE LEAVE VIETNAM? It's because the Democratic Party stopped the funding for the military. The American news media that covered the Vietnam War on a daily basis rarely covered what happened after our military left. The American public had very little knowledge of what happened.

What do you think will happen when we leave Iraq and come home? Of the approximately twenty five million Iraqi people how many will be killed, slaughtered? The opposition doesn't take prisoners, they kill them. Nancy Pelosi, Harry Reid, and General Murtha along with President Obama and several others will have this on their conscience.

The initial goal was to defeat Saddam and his regime. Second, we needed to militarily defeat the terrorists including the Shiites and Sunni that were creating havoc. Then when Iraq was stable enough we expect the elected politicians to work on developing a stable political climate and make the laws necessary to govern. Now it appears that most of the fighting has subsided and we and the Iraqis are fighting for democracy and establishing a democratic country. But the lull of fighting is fragile and ONLY depends on the USA being there to keep as much control as possible. Given the history between Iraq and Iran, Iraq is and will be vulnerable for some time especially with Iran's present regime and their assistance to the terrorists fighting in Iraq. The USA and President Bush did all we could to do what is right for Iraq. The problem is that the Democratic Party is now in control and they control 60% of the Congress. During the campaign Barrack Obama promised that there would be no American troops in Iraq by the end of 2009. Therefore a date was established for combat troops to leave Iraq by June 30, 2010. As of this writing the

American military has turned over most of the security to the Iraqi military. And as expected violence has returned to Iraq. Our troops are out of the Iraqi cities. Soon our troops will be out of Iraq. By pulling our troops out there will be immediate disaster for the Iraqi people as Al Qaeda and Iran will each create terrorist bombings to make it look like the blame will initially go against the Shiites and the Sunnis creating a civil war. This is the most complicated war in the history of mankind. WHY? Because the ideals of this war have to be overshadowed by the inevitable consequences that withdrawal of the American troops from Iraq and from the Middle East is of the greatest RISK to world peace ONLY because the USA and the western world is COMPLETELY DEPENDENT ON OIL. Leaving Iraq and the Middle East will cause such a vacuum that will create a DOMINO EFFECT of unprecedented proportions as the JIHAD MOVEMENT which has over 50% of the populations of the Muslim countries in the Middle East ready to unite as a snowball rolling down a steep hill. The JIHAD has leaders placed in the militaries of the Middle East countries that will make them unreliable to defend the leaders of each respective country if those leaders were to impose opposition to the JIHAD movement. Folks, this is complicated because the LAND THAT IS IRAQ IS SOME OF THE MOST IMPORTANT LAND IN THE WORLD AND IT WILL QUICKLY SPREAD INTO THE OTHER MIDDLE EAST COUNTRIES. Why? OIL/GAS!

This deserves repeating.

THE LAND THAT IS IRAQ AND THE MIDDLE EAST IS SOME OF THE MOST IMPORTANT LAND IN THE WORLD.

Folks, there was no oil/gas in Vietnam. The land that is Vietnam was not a security risk to the USA or the world.

For the record, there was very, very little uproar in the USA when several million Vietnamese were killed right after the USA left Vietnam. The party responsible, the Democrats, shed no tears. The majority of the American people did not know about the massacre as the news media did not cover that part of the war. Maybe there were just a few references to it. It was a silent event.

In 1973 the USA had an oil/gas crisis. Gas prices rose. There were long lines at the gasoline stations. The crisis ended. All was forgotten except for occasionally some rhetoric about being less dependent on foreign oil/gas. A few politicians said we should do something about it. Folks, 1973 that was 36 years ago! Nothing has been done. Reportedly the USA buys oil at a rate of 400 BILLION DOLLARS A YEAR FROM THE MIDDLE EAST. That's a lot of money in 36 years! And we are worst off today then we were in 1973. Every person who has "served" in the US Congress from 1973 to2009 should be held accountable as well as every President. Maybe these elected politicians "served" them selves because they sure did not "serve" the American people, did they? The 2007 US Congress passed a bill requiring cars to get 35 miles per gallon by the year 2020. That's 13 more years or 400 BILLION DOLLARS TIMES 13. That's a lot of money! Folks the technology is there to do it in 2 years! The US Congress should pass the law and any car manufacturer who does not want to comply can't sell their cars in the USA. Let's do something right! There has been some talk that the technology is there to get 50 miles per gallon.

President Bush said in the 2007 State of the Union speech that 75% of our oil/gas comes from the Middle East. He also said that we receive 10% of our oil/gas from Venezuela. That's 75% plus 10% equals 85% of our oil/gas!

SHOULD DEMOCRACY
BE COMPLEX?

Should every country in the world have a Democracy? It appeared to be the goal of President George W. Bush. Why? That appears to be a good question. Democracy is defined as the supreme power of a country is in the people who elect representatives to govern them. But do those elected representatives do what the people want them to do? Every time Congress votes on a bill has every representative surveyed the people they represent? NO! Possibly 5% of the representatives have surveyed their people. HELLO! This is NOT what is called representative government in a democracy. These representatives assume some power that in theory belongs to the people and without surveying the people's wishes on a bill they, the representative, are abusing the will of the people and vote according to their own wishes. So in actual practice the elected representatives do as they please. This is called democracy?

Impractical to survey the people before a vote is taken? Nonsense! With today's modern technology an elected representative should know when a bill is to be voted on and can inform their constituents and ask for their opinions. That is democracy!

But our Congress is complex. We have committees and subcommittees and chairmen/chairwomen and these individuals have become so powerful that they run/control the Congress. Nothing gets done unless these chairmen/chairwomen want to have it done. In theory every elected representative has equal power but in actual practice a powerful few determine what is voted on and strongly influence the voting. Congress is only as good as the people who are elected to it and the leadership of a powerful few. The acceptance or approval rating of Congress the last fifteen years has been in the 20% to 30% range which indicates the people are not happy with their performance. So in essence the powerful few along with the President rule the country and the WILL OF THE PEOPLE HAS NO VOTE!

One example of poor performance is that one of the political parties wanted to cut off the funding for 160,000 Americans who are in harms way, our military in Iraq, and that is not acceptable to most Americans. Yes, the Democratic Party would have and that is poor leadership. Another example was when the Democratic Party cut off the funding for our military in Vietnam and that resulted in three million people being killed. Where is the conscience of these politicians who do things like this, or don't they have any conscience?

(This author tells it like it is and does not favor one party over the other but speaks out according to the facts. This author is an independent registered voter and votes for the person who will do what is right for our country. To vote blindly for anyone because he/she is a Democrat or Republican is foolish. Democracy is based on responsible citizens).

In a democracy you can have too much change from one administration to the next which may lead to instability. For example, President Jimmy Carter almost made our military extinct and it took President Ronald Reagan to build it back up. Just imagine for a minute what if President Reagan would not have built our military back up the Soviet Union would still be intact. That would mean a strong Communist Soviet Union and Germany would still be divided and who knows maybe they would have attacked us. Folks, if we don't have a strong military it may jeopardize our democracy and freedom. A country should have continuity of its basic programs especially in defense.

Roger H. Ewing

We have been a democracy (actually it's a republic but everyone knows us as a democracy) for over 200 years and at times our government, the President and the Congress, has made it complex, confusing, and inadequate. If we can't get it right after 200 years why would we want to install a democracy in every country? There are other forms of government were the people have freedom. The USA may be the world's policeman but that doesn't mean we need a democracy in every country. The theory of a democracy is a wonderful thing but the actual practice when the politicians don't have integrity and continually lie to the people what do you really have? When the politicians spend all the peoples' money on pet projects and monuments to themselves what do you have?

What is wrong with a country having a strong monarchy where the people are free and have freedom? People can be free and have freedom without voting for their leaders. In the USA during the general election of November 2008 voting fraud was rampant. Some people were allowed to register over 70 times to vote. No one knows exactly how many fraudulent votes there really was. There could have been several hundred thousand fraudulent votes cast. It was recently reported that there were at least 400,000 fraudulent votes cast. The voting process leaves a lot to be desired. It could be made a clean process with identification requirements and address verification with finger printing to avoid fraud. Again, when you don't have integrity a politician can steal an election. A monarchy is defined as the supreme power is in one person. There have been many examples of good monarchies in history. An advantage would be long term planning of government programs especially in defense. Obviously there would not be billions of dollars in earmarks which is one factor in leading to bankrupting the USA. A monarchy could spend their money wisely and not be 12 trillion dollars in debt like the USA because of unwise spending of the politicians. A good monarch can lead his/her people for the common good. A bad monarch is usually overthrown or eliminated. Shouldn't we allow countries to have a good monarchy especially if that country has only had monarchies in their history? If we tinker too much in other countries we could easily mess up as we have a number of times. One example, we didn't like the Shah of Iran and we worked to expel him only to end up with a dictator.

BLITZKRIEG

The question of keeping a military base in Iraq has been brought up. The Democrats have said there will be no American base or troops in Iraq by the end of 2009. They have changed that date to August31, 2011. As violence has increased again and if it continues up to the anticipated date of withdrawal it will continue and even escalate after our American troops have left. We will get a real sense of the Iraqi political leadership and their future goals that if they do not negotiate a new date of withdrawal by the Spring of 2010 to keep our troops there to protect the gains made over the years of fighting. The problem is that this extension must be negotiated with President Barrack Obama who has painted himself into a corner by repeatedly saying our combat troops will leave no later than June 30, 2010. The problem is two-fold. One the political leadership in Iraq is dominated by the Shiites and they could gain by the USA leaving as Iran is Shiite and they could easily defeat the smaller and weaker Sunni population. The question then comes to will their religion be more important to them than their loyalty to their country of Iraq. Second in order for President Obama to agree to an extension to keep our troops in Iraq he would have to stand up to his own liberal Democratic Party who has demanded a withdrawal and end to the Iraq War and to bring our troops home now and would not stand for an extension. As of this date Barrack Obama has not stood up to the leaders in his party. He has not shown any sign of strength of character or leadership. You may recall that Barrack Obama said that we know him by the people he has around him. Some of the people, his advisors, which he appointed to advise him are considered radical or extremely liberal and it's either by his design or he just could not stand up and say no to them. So the answer to the problem of an extension is there is very little chance of it happening.

Also, another example of character or lack of a strong character is that usually when a person becomes President he informs the Congress and the American people what specifically his ideas or plans are based on his campaign promises. Well in Obama's case he campaigned on a stimulus package and health reform. But in both areas he did not spell out to the Congress or the American people what his ideas or plan was. This author through many years working as a management consultant to over 300 companies has experienced that people who have not made important decisions in their work life have a difficult time making them even when they are forced to. Remember Barrack Obama has not had to make decisions except as a lawyer in a court case or to organize a group of people. He has not run or managed a business or company of any size much less one of millions of dollars where he has to make important decisions daily.

Since World War II we have kept several American military bases in Germany and rightfully so for many reasons. Also, since the end of the Korean Conflict (War) we have kept American bases in South Korea. We need a presence for the security and defense of the regions which translates to a stronger security for the America homeland. Therefore it is not only vital for the region but for the USA to keep and maintain a military presence and base in Iraq.

The bottom line is that the survival of our nation is at stake. The character of our great nation must rise up and be heard. No more defeatism. We must draw from the strength of character of our great leaders of the past who saved our great country in their plight as we are now. Draw from the strength of courage from John Adams, George Washington, Thomas Jefferson, Benjamin Franklin, Teddy Roosevelt, FDR (even though he made many mistakes he got the job done), and

Ronald Reagan. These men conquered the demons of their time. Now we must conquer the demons of our time.

This book is a call to action for all Americans to understand the enormity of the problem. Again, this book is a call for all Americans to understand that we cannot leave Iraq. By leaving Iraq we are defeated! Without the oil/gas we are defeated! Again 75% of our oil/gas comes from Iraq and the Middle East and we cannot live without it. If we leave Iraq the Middle East will be defeated. THE BOTTOM LINE IS WE NEED THE MIDDLE EAST AND IRAQ MORE THAN THEY NEED US.

IF THE MIDDLE EAST IS CONTROLLED BY THE JIHAD THIS WOULD RESULT IN THE DOWNFALL OF THE USA.

THE WORLD CAN CHANGE IN AN IN-STANT.

Here is what will happen. The American military will come home. The Shiites supported by Iran/JIHAD immediately attack the Sunni and in blitzkrieg fashion win overwhelmingly. Then the Kurds are defeated. Then what appears to be total shock and awe to most of the Western world but not to those in the Middle East, the Middle East succumbs to the Shiites, or in reality to JIHAD.

Walid Shoebat, a former JIHAD terrorist, in his book wrote and verbalized to the media that given an opportunity to vote the people of the countries of the Middle East would support JIHAD movement. Over 50% of the people in each of the Middle East countries would do so. That includes Saudi Arabia, Egypt, Jordan, Syria, Iran, Turkey, and others.

ONCE IT STARTS THERE IS THE POINT OF NO RETURN! WE CANNOT LET IT START! WHY RISK IT IF YOU DON'T HAVE TO! STAY IN IRAQ!

The American military is back in the good old USA. This is how it will be. The leadership in Washington will say we have no business going back to Iraq. Visualize the American military is in the USA and fighting escalates in Iraq, the American military will not go back. Period.

YOU HAVE TO GRASP THIS POINT!

THIS IS THE TURNING POINT OF THE WORLD!

SO IN A SHORT PERIOD OF TIME THE JIHAD TERRORISTS WOULD CONTROL IRAQ AND THE MIDDLE EAST. THAT MEANS THAT

THE JIHAD TERRORISTS CONTROL THE OIL/GAS OF THE MIDDLE EAST.

In plain English the Jihad terrorists are the Islamic Muslim terrorists and their goal is to destroy the USA.

That's 75% of the oil/gas that we depend on plus Venezuela won't sell us their 10% gas anymore, that's 85%, for our everyday living and for the defense of the USA. That oil/gas will not be available anymore. We will only have 15% for everything!

Russia won't sell us any. Mexico doesn't have enough to make up the difference. We in the USA cannot make up the difference. Our emergency supply won't last long and it will be reserved for the military. We can't get oil/gas anywhere! Alaska has plenty but it's off limits and has not begun to be discovered. We have plenty of oil/gas off of our coasts but that has been off limits and not discovered. How long can the USA last/survive without oil/gas?

LIFE AS WE KNOW IT WILL BE AT A STANDSTILL!

All the JIHAD terrorists have to do is wait us out and then attack. The terrorists are not peaceful people. The terrorists' goal is to destroy the USA, kill Americans, which they have said repeatedly. People who read "Mein Kampf" never believed they would try to conquer the world. The terrorists will try and without oil/gas we will be helpless. This is THE DOWNFALL OF THE USA.

Without 85% of our oil/gas and with JIHAD in control of the Middle East it is safe for Communist China to attack.

CHINA ATTACKS THE USA

With the USA vulnerable Communist China attacks the USA. This sounds as ridiculous as Japan attacks the USA on December 7th, 1941. Who would have thought it? Doesn't sound as ridiculous now does it? How did it happen? President Franklin D. Roosevelt and the Congress avoided the signs of a possible attack while they were busy with the economy. Their elitist attitude was that no one would attack the USA. Does it sound familiar? In 2010 the economy is struggling and our President Obama and the Congress believes no one will attack us again. Our President Obama and his Attorney General have weakened our intelligence services to the point where another attack on us is possible. The signs are there will we heed them. Remember that third grade class? Well they can add 1994 plus 15 years adds up to 2009. That's the magic date that the Communist Chinese leadership set as being ready for war. Anytime after 2009 we are vulnerable to an attack. We seem to underestimate the reality of what a Communist country wants to do mainly that they want to establish a Communist government around the world. President Harry Truman did not understand that with Russia after World War II. He should have listened to General George Patton. Remember, General Patton won more land against a greater enemy in the shortest period of time than anyone in the history of the world. Who are the leaders of Communist China ready to go to war with? Their number one enemy as they established in 1994. They believe this is their opportunity to gain control of the world. They believe that they can control the Muslim/JIHAD and that Russia is no longer a threat to them. This is their time!

Why have a war? If you have read a Bible the Old Testament talks of continuous wars over the ages. The primary reason for going to war was religion. This has held true even in modern times. Also, to conquer the world has been closely aligned with various religions.

China, in its entire history, has developed no concept of limited government, or protections of individual rights, or independence for the judiciary and the media. It has never in its history operated on any notion of the consent of the governed. The Communist Chinese leaders don't like democratic ideas.

A democracy is a weak form of governing and controlling the masses/people.

FOLKS REALITY IS THAT THE LEADERS OF COMMUNIST CHINA DON'T LIKE US. COMMUNISM IS LIKE JIHAD THEY WANT TO TAKE OVER THE WORLD. THAT'S A FACT.

So What Will Happen?

When our oil/gas runs out, the Islamic Muslim JIHAD terrorists will attack the USA. These JIHAD terrorist cells that are in the USA will create havoc all over our country. They will be joined by a hoard of JIHAD from Iran and the Middle East. Then Communist Chinese will attack us. Americans won't be able to respond. Local governments won't have the resources to maintain law and order or any other services. State and federal governments are unable to provide any services. State National Guard units won't be able to respond as they left most of their equipment in Iraq. We will be fighting in the streets of our cities and towns all across the USA. Millions of American men, women, and children will be killed. Cities and towns will be destroyed. The American way of life will be destroyed This is reality because the enemy will overwhelm us.

FOLKS, HAS OUR GOVERNMENT GIVEN YOU ANY INSTRUCTIONS ON WHAT TO DO IF WE ARE ATTACKED? ARE YOU AWARE OF ANY PREPARATIONS TO DEFEND US ONCE THE ENEMY HAS ARRIVED IN THE USA?

Our Congress won't help.

The United Nations won't help.

The great debate over health care will be over. No one will have any.

The great debate over global warming will be over. No one will care.

The great debate over carbon dioxide will be over. The parts of the USA that have coal fired plants for energy will be better off than those dependent on natural gas plants. Why? The natural gas plants will be shut down for lack of oil/gas. This debate has really become a no brainer. The USA has enough coal for the next 250 years, and it's cleaner than ever before. There presently is ongoing research to make it even cleaner. In the meantime, natural gas prices have tripled since 1999 and prices are going even higher. And natural gas is dependent on foreign imports. Nuclear energy produces a waste that no one knows what to do with it. The thought of storing the nuclear waste in Nevada was the plan but that has lost favor because the science reportedly was flawed and transporting it to Yucca Mountain is too hazardous. Wind turbine energy is not dependable and needs a backup energy system and has been reported to be more expensive than initially thought. Even Boone Pickens once the self appointed spokesman for wind energy has backed off of it. But several companies are pushing it to make a huge profit.

The Environmental Protection Agency (EPA) won't protect us. They and the politicians have kept our oil/gas in the ground.

WE ARE THE SUPER POWER BUT WITHOUT OIL/GAS OUR WEAPONS SYSTEMS DON'T MOVE, AND ARE OBSOLETE, USELESS. IN FACT AMERICANS AREN'T MOVING. WHAT LITTLE THERE IS WILL IMEDIATELY BE RATIONED AND CONTROLLED BY THE FEDERAL GOVERNMENT. REMEMBER WE HAVE LOST 85% OF THE OIL/GAS THAT WE IMPORT. THIS HAS RESULTED IN AN ABRUPT CHANGE IN THE AMERICAN WAY OF LIFE. THE USA WILL COME TO A SCREECHING HALT. ONCE OUR OIL/GAS HAS BEEN CUT

OFF ALL OUR ENEMIES HAVE TO DO IS WAIT THREE MONTHS OR SIX MONTHS UNTIL WE HAVE RUN OUT AND THEN THEY WILL ATTACK.

Our economy depends on the transportation of goods. Most goods are transported by large trucks. These large trucks need plenty of gas/oil to move the products to the retail stores. Where will the fuel needed come from? There will be food shortages all over the country. Imagine for a moment what life would be without oil/gas. How dependent we are on driving for so many of our basic necessitates. Gasoline stations will not have gas to sell. You will not be driving to work or anywhere else. The 300 million American people will stop cheering for their sports heroes and entertainment idols and face the reality that the government has failed them. The American people won't blame themselves for not having paid attention to the ineptness of their elected leaders

If you think this scenario is flawed ask yourself these questions.

1. Do you have a 90 day food supply on hand?

2. Do you have a 90 day supply of gas on hand?

3. How are you going to heat your house in the winter if you are dependent on natural gas?

4. If you don't need to worry about the first 3 questions how are you going to defend yourself against those who will fight you for what you have?

Remember we left Iraq and everything SNOWBALLED from there.

FOLKS, THIS IS FOR REAL! IT'S NO GAME! This author was in Europe after World War II and saw the devastation first hand. Cities and towns were 80% to 90% destroyed from day and night bombing. There was very little left. Houses were in rumble. Food was scarce. Shelter was scarce. This was the civilian population not the military as the military was nonexistent having been destroyed. And this author has seen the devastation of Japan when two bombs destroyed Hiroshima and Nagasaki. You haven't seen anything yet because that was 1945, today's bombs and weapons systems are many times more powerful.

What Can We Do Now?

We need to wake up to reality. Reality is the JIHAD terrorists will cut off our oil/gas supply. Reality is the JIHAD terrorists want to conquer us, kill us, and everything we as a country stand for. We need to stand up and be Americans again. Americans stand for good in the world and we have accomplished so very much good.

There have been many great empires in the history of the world and they conquered their enemies and consumed them into an empire but the USA didn't build an empire to conquer and consume their enemies but to defeat those as needed to attempt peace on earth. For some reason GOD has chosen the USA to be the world's policeman and we must be good stewards of our responsibility, and if we fail disaster may strike all over the world.

Did 9/11 happen because GOD wanted to awaken Americans to the reality of the threat of evil which is the JIHAD movement to destroy the USA and the western civilizations? It appears that GOD has blessed the USA in many ways over the last two centuries and wants us to continue HIS work, of good over evil.

Folks, as Americans we need to wake up to this reality!

We need to call our Congress representatives NOW! Tell them you don't want our military to leave Iraq. Tell them too much is at stake. The survival of the USA is at stake. Simply tell them that the Iraqi people need us to protect them from the onslaught that will occur if we leave. Tell them that the Shiites who are in control of the Iraqi government must extend our stay in Iraq. We must insist on it.

There have been over three thousand Americans killed in Iraq but that number is small compared to the MILLIONS of Americans who will be killed NOT IF BUT WHEN the Islamic JIHAD Muslims terrorists and the Communist Chinese come to the USA!

Call your Congress representatives NOW before they come!

Folks every American life lost in war is precious. But to put things in proper perspective these men and women were fighting for a cause. In comparison, the following people were not fighting for a cause. Each year in the USA there have been between 17,000 to 18,000 alcohol related car/truck deaths in the USA. That's drunk driving deaths. That's deaths caused by drunk drivers. Since the Iraq war started in 2003 there have been over 85,000 people killed in the USA by drunk drivers. The Iraq war has taken over 3,000 in that period of time. Should there be a national uproar against our politicians who have done very little to restrict alcohol? It appears that every time a politician wants a new program they want to tax cigarettes more. Just maybe if alcohol were to be taxed more than just maybe there would be less drunk drivers. But the odds are that the politicians drink more alcohol than they smoke cigarettes therefore alcohol is safe from the scrutiny that cigarettes have gotten over the years.

One thing we should not do is have a repeat of the 1992 Presidential election. President H. W. Bush ran for re-election against Bill Clinton. A third party candidate, Ross Perot, emerged. His straight talk about the economy which had a downturn captured the minds and hearts of the idealist and he received about 15% to 20% of the vote which this author believes kept Bush from winning the election. If a third party candidate were to mount a strong campaign in 2012 that would almost guarantee Obama a second term. That assumes that Americans are still in control of the USA.

COMING OF THE END-TIME

American politicians have helped cause the downfall and destruction of Jerusalem and Israel. For over two decades the USA has been pressuring Israel to give up more and more land to create a Palestine state. This Palestine state is currently controlled by Hamas which is one of the leading groups in the JIHAD movement. And Hamas is either controlled by Iran or has strong ties to them. As the land of Israel is shrinking rockets can now attack every part of the country. Jerusalem is vulnerable to attack and the present day negotiations to divide this most holy city by several parties including the USA will bring the world closer to the END-TIME. Remember the WORD OF GOD! Whatever country has a hand in dividing Jerusalem which weakens it and thereby helps in its destruction will be destroyed.

The most prolific and accurate predictor of future events Nostradamus in the 16th century also predicted the 2012 events. Most people who have studied the events of 2012 and the END-TIME believe the "Anti-Christ" will be a Muslim. Nostradamus, however, in his writings about 2012 and the END-TIME depicts his prediction like this. The "Anti-Christ" is with an American eagle and its right before 2012. Nostradamus in all of his writings/predictions over 500 years ago only wrote two words in English. That's amazing in itself as the United States of America was discovered in 1492 as we all know. His prediction came in the 1500s reference to the 2012 events. The only two words in English that Nostradamus wrote were "one male" in association right before and with 2012. The meaning translates into the number one male in the USA who is a Muslim or possibly born to a Muslim during the two or three years before 2012. This appears to be Barrack Obama. Could it be? Think about it! He has put intense pressure on Israel to give more land to the Muslims and he wants to divide Jerusalem and give parts of it to the Muslims. Obama has put Israel "between a rock and a hard place" Iran is almost at the point of having nuclear weapons which it said they will use against Israel as they want to destroy them. So Israel needs to attack Iran now but does not know for the first time since 1948 if the USA and namely President Obama will back them up. Israel can not go it alone anymore as the JIHAD would unite against them. But what if Obama says that Israel provoked a war against Iran/ Muslims and orders our military to attack Israel. Would our military obey the orders? Obama wants to establish a civilian force that is as strong as our military. Is that to counter our military if they don't obey his orders? Obama in all of his speeches around the world has said that America is a bad country. Many Americans believe he is changing/transforming America into a socialist country with a weakened military, weakened CIA, and weakened freedoms.

But that seems preposterous! Barrack went to college in California where he admitted he did drugs, then went to Columbia University, and then to Harvard University. Since Columbia and Harvard are expensive to attend possibly he got some financial help. He definitely has been living the American dream. But his association with radicals for most of his adult life who have a history of wanting to overthrow our government or do damage to our government speaks volumes about him. But as hard as it is to believe Nostradamus in the 1500s predicted the assassination of John Kennedy, World War I, and World War II and the bombings of the twin towers on 9/11. This is scary stuff!

Bible prophecy predicts that when Jerusalem is attacked by the many Muslim nations there will be destruction throughout the Middle East. A NUCLEAR BOMB WILL BE EXPLODED! The Bible refers to this as the GREAT WAR. Before it's all over at least one-half of the world's population will be killed. One of the countries involved in this GREAT WAR has a military of 200 million people. What country could have a military this BIG? China? Russia is also involved in the GREAT WAR on the side of the JIHAD. The first NUCLEAR BOMB will explode in Saudi Arabia. It's not clear but this NUCLEAR BOMB is dropped by either Russia, or Pakistan, or Turkey.

At the end it's not a question of who wins but who survives. The final curtain is when THE LORD JESUS CHRIST COMES DOWN FROM HEAVEN AND DEFEATS THE ENEMY. THAT FOLKS IS BIBLE PROPHECY. (This is just a quick synopsis of the GREAT WAR and the END-TIME, the BIBLE gives you all the details).

You may have noticed that the USA is not mentioned in the last moments of the END-TIME because by interfering in the destruction of Jerusalem the USA was destroyed earlier.

BUT

GOD HAS GIVEN MAN (MANKIND) A FREE WILL. MAN (MANKIND) CAN DO WHAT IS RIGHT AND WHAT IS GOOD. IT'S UP TO THE PRESENT LEADERS OF THE WORLD TO DO WHAT IS RIGHT AND WHAT IS GOOD FOR OUR WORLD. THEY CAN DESTROY IT OR PRESERVE IT. GOD CREATED OUR WORLD AND MAN (MANKIND) CAN DESTROY IT.

BUT

Roger H. Ewing

WE KNOW WITH THE AMERICAN MILITARY
AT FULL STRENGTH IN IRAQ THE MIDDLE
EAST WILL NOT FALL AND WE WILL CON-
TINUE TO RECEIVE THE OIL/GAS WE DES-
PERATELY NEED TO CONTINUE TO MAKE
PROGRESS AND MOST IMPORTANT TO BE
THE GREAT FORCE WE ARE IN THE WORLD
TO MAINTAIN A BALANCE FOR WHAT IS
RIGHT AND WHAT IS GOOD.

BUT

Roger H. Ewing

WE CANNOT MAINTAIN A FULL STRENGTH MILITARY IN IRAQ AND AROUND THE WORLD WITH OUR PRESENT ACTIVE MILITARY MANPOWER. IT IS ABSOLUTELY NECESSARY TO INCREASE OUR ACTIVE MILITARY MANPOWER TO FIVE MILLION PERSONNEL IMMEDIATELY.

THE PROBLEM IS WE NEED TO DO IT WITH OUR PRESENT CONGRESS. WE CANNOT WAIT FOR THE MID-TERM ELECTIONS IN NOVEMBER 2010 WHEN THE CONGRESS WILL HAVE MORE REPUBLICANS AND THEY DON'T TAKE OFFICE UNTIL JANUARY 2011. THIS CURRENT DEMOCRATIC PARTY WHICH CONTROLS BOTH HOUSES OF CONGRESS AND THIS LIBERAL PRESIDENT MUST RESPOND AND DO WHAT IS RIGHT FOR THE USA AND FOR THE WORLD. IT'S THE ONLY WAY WE ARE NOT DESTROYED IN 2012.

THE CLOCK IS TICKING, EVERY SECOND IS PRECIOUS, EVERY MINUTE. ARE WE USING OUR TIME WORKING TOWARDS OUR NATIONAL DEFENSE GOALS OR JUST WASTING PRECIOUS TIME?

GOD HELP US TO UNDERSTAND THE REALITY THAT IS TO BESET US.

WAKE UP AMERICA! WAKE UP!

NOTABLE CHARACTERS

JOHN MCCAIN, III

American Patriot

POW – Prisoner of War – 51/2 years – 1967 –1973

United States Senator -- 1987 to Present

Ran unsuccessful for President of USA

Graduated almost last in graduating class at Naval Academy

In this author's opinion McCain did not run a good campaign in his run for President of USA in 2008. Even though he selected Sarah Palin as his running mate which energized his campaign he did not protect her. McCain for the most part played defense, his offense was poor or lacking. His opponents, Obama and Biden, were attacking Palin as inexperienced and lacking international knowledge. Well Obama lacked both. Biden who became a United States Senator in January 1973 while McCain was still a POW in North Vietnam vigorously attacked McCain and Palin during the campaign. Biden is known for continuously saying off the wall crazy things which has him "putting his foot in his mouth". A case could be made that Americans feared Biden as President more than Palin. After all Biden received only 1% of the votes/delegates during the Democratic Party Primary. And this was his second attempt at running for President and he had been in the Senate for 35 years! Americans don't have much confidence in Joe Biden. McCain would not attack Biden claiming he was a good friend. This was a major mistake McCain made and it may have made a difference. McCain also stayed away from mentioning Jeremiah Wright. McCain received 46% of the votes. You add 4% more McCain could have won.

JOE BIDEN, JR.

Biden finished in the lower 25% of his graduating class from college.

Biden received 5 student deferments to avoid military service during Vietnam. Then when he was to go he claimed he had asthma as a teenager – if that were the case why wouldn't he have brought the asthma up originally?

United States Senator from Delaware since 1973.

Biden strongly supported Bosnian War.

Opposed Gulf War/ Desert Storm in 1991.

Voted for Iraq War Resolution in 2002.

Biden wanted to divide Iraq into 3 ethnic states in November 2006.

Kurds, Shiites, Sunnis.

Ran for President in 1988 and 2008. Receives 1% of the vote from his own party.

Joe Biden is best known nationally for putting his foot in his mouth for his idiotic mumblings

NEWT GINGRICH

Speaker of the House of Representatives – 1995 –1999

Contract with America -- In the November 1994 elections Republicans gained 54 seats and took control of the House of Representatives for the first time since 1954.

Resigned after 1998 elections.

American Solutions for Winning the Future

Newt Gingrich appears to be one of the more intelligent politicians. Has a great success record in getting things done but like all achievers he stepped on some toes of people who had selfish ambitions and who didn't understand and appreciate Gingrich's accomplishments.

HILLARY CLINTON

Would Hillary Clinton be President today if it weren't for her husband Bill Clinton? When Bill was President for 8 years he became powerful and influential. Bill it was reported was a Rhodes Scholar. Bill's intelligence and influence led the Democratic Party to change the way the Democrats choose their presidential candidate. Under the old system if a presidential candidate won a state he/she received most of the delegates but under Bill's new system a candidate coming in second could receive almost as many delegates as the winner. Remember 2008 when Hillary won the state of Texas and barely received a few more delegates than Barrack Obama. Hillary also won Ohio and Pennsylvania. That's three big states and only a little gain in delegates.

Hillary opened many Americans' eyes that she was not just a former President's wife but intelligent in her own right. She held her own in the debates and proved to be capable. She would have been a natural Secretary of Health and Human Services with her strong background/interest in health care/insurance. For Hillary to be Secretary Of State is a stretch.

In my opinion the office of Secretary of State requires an experienced international statesman/woman. Hillary's husband Bill can't help when it comes to international statesmanship as that was his weakest area of expertise.

MITT ROMNEY

Graduated Valedictorian at BYU -- Bachelors Degree

Graduated with Honors – top 5% of class -- Harvard

For Masters Degree

Successful turnaround of 2002 Winter Olympics

Successful Businessman

Governor of Massachusetts -- 2003 – 2007

Romney appears to be one of the most intelligent politi-cians.

Fair And Balanced News Reporters/ Analysts

Brit Hume -- Fox News -- intelligent and tells it like it is, worth listening to.

Bill o'Reilly -- King of Cable News

Glenn Beck -- Crusader for the U. S. Constitution

Charles Krauthammer -- Newspaper Columnist worth listening to, knows what he is talking about

Andrew Napolitano -- a real expert on the U. S. Constitution

THE HOUSING CRISIS
AND RECESSION

HENRY PAULSON and BEN BERNANKE

Henry "Hank" Paulson received his Bachelors Degree majoring in English. He continued his education and received a MBA.

He spent most of his years prior to being named Secretary of the Treasury as an investment banker -- 1974 –2006.

An investment banker doesn't deal with the ins and outs of the economy, or interest rates, or unemployment rates, or business cycles. An investment banker makes deals/ investments for his company and or clients.

Paulson became CEO of Goldman Sachs where he personally made a fortune, anywhere from 100 million to 700 million, it has been reported. And somehow President George W. Bush appointed him to be the Secretary of the Treasury.

So the scenario is that the Congress over many years time allowed Fannie Mae and Freddy Mac to guarantee home mortgages through mortgage companies/banks to people who would have a hard time in paying the monthly mortgage but because of the leniency were approved to buy a home. So when defaults started and eventually started to add up the federal government had to bail out Fannie and Freddy.

Because some wise money guy created REITs, Real Estate Investment Trusts, the mortgages were combined and sold and resold and lots of people made tons of money until too many defaults happened. This caused the banks holding some of these mortgages to have toxic assets. This created an atmosphere that the banks decided not to loan money to customers. Basically it froze the financial lending markets. The result of not loaning any money began to create problems to businesses and they in turn started laying off employees.

For the poor buyer of homes and many had ARMs, adjustable rate mortgages, their monthly payments in many cases started increasing and this became the major reason the owners of those homes went into default and ended up losing their homes.

Hank Paulson, the English major, decided he needed help so he called in Ben Bernanke the Federal Reserve Chairman.

Ben Bernanke, the economics major, who has had an obsession with the Great Depression of 1929, accepted the challenge of solving this financial crisis. Bernanke who had extensively studied the Great Depression came up with his theory of solving the crisis. He decided to give billions of dollars to the investment banks and to the largest banks in the country. This should increase the confidence of these banks to loan money and create the flow of money into the economy. So Bernanke and Paulson gave the billions of dollars to the parties that through their excessive greed played a large part in creating the problem. We all hope that it works.

But was this the greatest financial disaster since the Great Depression or the normal up and down turn of the market?

In 2008 the prime interest rate was 3.25% and the unemployment rate was at 6.6%. In September 2009 the prime interest rate was still at 3.25% and the unemployment rate was at 9.7%

If we compare those rates to the rates during Jimmy Carter's presidency which had an prime interest rate of 21.5% and an unemployment rate of 7.5% shouldn't this be considered a much worst time for the American people? When Jimmy

Carter took office the prime interest rate was 6.25% and through his policies the rate was 21.5% went he left. Carter left office in January 1981. The prime interest rate stayed high until 1988 when it was 10.5%. When George H. W. Bush left office in January 1993 the rate was 8.5%. Then when Bill Clinton left office the rate was 9%.

During Jimmy Carter's term when the prime interest rate was 21.5% the banks were not lending any money. Money was frozen and it took about eight years before banks felt confident loaning again. There was no 700 billion dollar government bailout as in November 2008. The economy in the 1980s moved along without going over the 7.5% unemployment rate. Probably most important without a large government bailout it didn't add to the huge deficit/debt as in 2008 and 2009 with the government Stimulus package of another almost 800 billion dollars. It is noted that the large Stimulus package has not resulted in a large number of hiring in the private sector but only in the federal government. And only a small fraction of the Stimulus money has been spent in eight months! If this were the worst recession since 1929 the unemployment rate would be much higher and the prime interest rate would have soared. Private businesses are complaining that money is still very tight and they cannot get any loans since the bailout a year later.

Was there a simple solution? It was reported that 92% of homeowners paid their monthly mortgages on time. And it was widely known that most of the 8% were on ARMs and once the ARMs adjusted upward creating a larger monthly payment those homeowners would have a difficult time making those payments. So when the defaults started the government led by Paulson and Bernanke could have frozen the ARMs keeping them at the level where the homeowners were able to pay. This would have been the logical thing to do except that would mean that the greedy mortgage companies/banks would not be making the huge profits. Also, the mortgage companies/banks could have adjusted their payment schedules whereby the homeowner who had difficulty in making their payments could pay half and additional time could have been added on to the contract. Contracts can be re-negotiated with consent of the parties. Both parties involved had incentive to do that. Homeowners who were in good faith should have been allowed to keep their homes. Why did the mortgage companies/banks foreclose so quickly only to accumulate thousands of homes which they couldn't sell? As it turned out these homes became toxic assets on the banks balance sheets. And greed prevailed! And Paulson and Bernanke added 700 billion dollars to our debt/deficit that we did not have to. Oh, by the way 95 banks have failed in 2009 so far.

There has not been a President who has had a deep knowledge and understanding of monetary policy and financial policies at least since 1900. In fairness to George W. Bush he depended on his Secretary of the Treasury, Hank Paulson, and the Federal Reserve Chairman Ben Bernanke to advise him. Did Paulson and Bernanke over react? Was it necessary to spend the billions? Or was there another agenda? Paulson was the CEO of Goldman Sachs and they received billions of dollars. Also, AIG received billions of dollars with a large chunk of their money ending up at Goldman Sachs. Even if they had to pay the money back eventually a company or person can make a ton of money using those billions, that money. Should the Inspector General investigate the bailout and what happened to all of the 700 billions?

ACCORDING TO THE NATIONAL BUREAU OF ECONOMIC RESEARCH THERE WERE 10 BUSINESS CYCLE EXPANSIONS AND CONTRACTIONS FROM 1945 TO 2001.

Health Care Reform

For a year Barrack Obama said there were 46 or 47 million Americans that did not have health care/insurance. Then in a speech to both houses of congress and to a national television audience said there were 30 million Americans uninsured eliminating 16 or 17 million people presumed to be the illegal aliens. So for a year did Obama call the illegal aliens Americans?

Of the 30 million uninsured Americans approximately 20 million are between 20 and 35 years of age who could afford to buy health insurance but choose not to. That leaves approximately 10 million who can not afford health insurance.

So all the hoopla is about insuring 10 million people. Why? Could there be a hidden Agenda? Maybe President Obama wants to initiate a new system which transforms the whole health care/insurance system to be a government run health care system. Many of Obama's advisors and supporters have said once they get their foot in the door it will eventually take over the whole system. A government run health care system has many negatives.

For a year Barrack Obama has said that the waste and fraud of the present health care system, Medicare and Medicaid, will pay for 2/3 of the 900 billion or one trillion dollars program he wants to implement. That's 2/3 of 900 billion or 600 billion. What person would allow 600 billion to be wasted for a year without correcting the problem? Most Americans don't believe there is 600 billion waste or fraud in the present health care system.

Almost everyone agrees that the health care/insurance system needs to be reformed.

President Obama said that the AMA, American Medical Association, supports his plan, but in a survey of medical doctors 65% said they did not support his plan.

Also, initially Obama said that the AARP, American Association of Retired Persons, supported his plan, but AARP came out on national television claiming they did not support his plan.

In August 2009 during the many town hall meetings the American people spoke their minds and overwhelmingly did not support Obama's plan.

Also, national polls in September 2009 showed that the American people did not support Obama's plan.

But in spite of all the opposition the Democratic Party which control both houses of congress will cram a health care/insurance plan down the American's throats. That folks is the Obama way of doing things! Obama does not care what the majority of Americans want as long as he gets what he wants.

Oh, by the way those 16 or 17 million illegal aliens they will get health care but they do not have to pay for it. All they have to do is to go to a hospital and they will receive health care. The federal government has mandated that anyone that shows up at a hospital will receive health care. Judge Andrew Napolitano has said the Supreme Court has made this clear.

So why is anyone buying health insurance?

Everyone who pays for health insurance is also paying for those that do not have it, legal or illegal.

So in reality we need to add 46 or 47 million people to the health care system without adding any additional medical doctors. And 25% of our medical doctors are nearing retirement age. Logic and common sense speaks volumes that there is and will be a huge shortage of medical doctors and that equates to rationing and long waits for appointments. Many experts have said that senior citizens will be hurt the most and this generation was called the "greatest generation" because they have given so much and sacrificed so much to America especially during World War II and now in their senior years they are going to be sacrificed by the Obama government. Reality folks! That's what Obama's advisor has said. So Obama's plan wants to provide health care to the younger generation who have not contributed to a health plan in lieu of the seniors who have contributed to the health care plan all of their lives.

NOTABLE QUOTATIONS

The results do not justify the means if you have achieved them by any means except through HONEST work/effort -- for those who have a conscious.

Thinking is one thing no one has ever been able to tax.
Charles Franklin Kettering

Right is right, even if everyone is against it; and wrong is wrong , even if everyone is for it.
William Penn

Thinking is the hardest work there is, which is probably the reason so few engage in it.

Henry Ford

Don't use time or words carelessly, neither can be retrieved.

No man is justified in doing evil on the ground of expedience.

Theodore Roosevelt

Character is that which reveals moral purpose, exposing the class of things a man chooses or avoids.

Aristotle

Don't let the fear of striking out get in the way of your success.

Babe Ruth

Thomas Edison discovered over 1000 ways that didn't work until he came up with the light bulb.

Have high standards and values – whatever standards and values you have tell people what you are.

Think about what the consequences of your actions may be. Do you want to pay the price?

Your INTEGRITY represents what you are.

The world is governed more by appearances than by realities, so that it is fully as necessary to seem to know something as to know it.

Daniel Webster

The reason some men do not succeed is because their wishbone is where their backbone ought to be.

VOTE. It is very important that you vote. Vote in the primaries. Vote in the general elections. VOTE.

Better to bend than to break.

Learn how to gather information. Learn how to understand the facts to make the right decision.

Praise in public. Criticize in private.

It may take a lifetime to build a reputation which you could lose in minutes.

Become THE person who has the ideas. Learn how to think.

Genius is one percent inspiration and ninety- nine percent perspiration.

Thomas Edison

Whatever you are trying to avoid won't go away until you confront it.

One thing we learn from history is that history repeats itself.

Anger and intolerance are the twin enemies of correct understanding.

Mahatma Gandhi

Read the U. S. Constitution.

FREEDOM – Never take FREEDOM for granted. NEVER.

Honor those who have served in the military.

Don't be afraid to say, "I don't know"

The gem cannot be polished without friction, nor man perfected without trials.

Chinese Proverb

Never compromise your integrity. Never.

Beware of the person who has nothing to lose.

Others can stop you temporarily, only you can do it permanently.

You can't escape the responsibility of tomorrow by evading it today.

Abraham Lincoln

Pay attention to the details.

Be a good loser. Be a good winner.

Inspiration -- Ronald Reagan was a senior citizen before he was President.

There is no way of know before experiencing.

Leave everything a little better than you found it.

After all is said and done, much is said and little is done.

Don't take yourself too seriously.

Learn to NEGOTIATE. It is a skill you will use the rest of your life.

If it is the TRUTH what does it matter who says it.

Purpose is a source of energy and direction.

Discover what moves you!

Learn statistics and numbers. When reading about statistics and numbers in newspapers or other print medium, be careful and try to understand what is really said. Statistics can be easily manipulated, misleading.

Educators should be chosen not merely for their special qualifications, but more for their personality and their character, because we teach more by what we are than by what we teach.

> Will Durant

Look at every RAINBOW!

Behold the turtle, he makes progress ONLY when he sticks his neck out.

COMMUNICATION – is vital. Learn how to communicate to say EXACTLY what you want to say.

Learn to stay in control under pressure.

How do you want to be remembered?
For good? For evil?

Common sense is the knack of seeing things as they are,
and doing things as they ought to be done.
Stowe

Your mind responds to what you allow to enter it.

GARBAGE IN GARBAGE OUT. Be careful.

Self-respect and honour cannot be protected by others.
They are for each individual himself or herself to guard.
Mahatma Gandhi

Let us have faith that right makes might, and in that faith
let us to the end dare to do our duty as we understand it.
Abraham Lincoln

In matter of principle, stand like a rock; in matters of taste
swim with the current.
Thomas Jefferson

Never do anything against conscience even if the state
demands it.
Albert Einstein

God's gift to us is life. Our gift to God is what we become.
God measures our success in what values/standards we have
and not in how much money we have acquired.

About the Author

Roger Ewing was ONE of America's first international inspectors of weapons systems and disarmament as he participated in the First International Disarmament Exercise as a Division Inspector. Roger learned the ability to analyze a country's capability to wage war. He also predicted the fall of the Soviet Union from within 16 years before it happened. Roger has a Bachelors Degree from Bowling Green State University in Ohio. He received a Masters Degree from the University of Southern California and did his PhD work at Arizona State University. Roger was an Air Force Officer and a Management Consultant for many years.